STO

FRIENDS
OF A

D0934836

8L

PATRICK EWING

CENTER OF ATTENTION

By Howard Reiser

CHILDRENS PRESS®
CHICAGO

Photo Credits

Cover, ©McDonough/Focus on Sports; 5, 6, ©Brian Drake/Sportschrome; 9, UPI/Bettmann; 11, AP/Wide World; 12, ©Jerry Wachter/Focus on Sports; 14, AP/Wide World; 17, UPI/Bettmann; 19, ©Jerry Wachter/ Focus on Sports; 20, AP/Wide World; 23, 25, UPI/Bettmann; 26, ©David L. Johnson/Sports Photo Masters, Inc.; 28, 31, AP/Wide World; 32, Focus on Sports; 35, ©Jonathan Kirn/Sports Photo Masters, Inc.; 37, ©Brian Drake/ Sportschrome; 39, AP/Wide World; 40, ©Vincent Manniello/Sportschrome; 43, Focus on Sports; 44, AP/Wide World

Project Editors: Shari Joffe and Mark Friedman
Design: Beth Herman Design Associates
Photo Editor: Jan Izzo

Acknowledgements

The author would like to thank retired basketball great Jack "Dutch" Garfinkel, former Knicks coach Fuzzy Levane, and the Elias Sports Bureau.

Library of Congress Cataloging-in-Publication Data

Reiser, Howard.
    Patrick Ewing: center of attention / by Howard Reiser.
        p. cm. – (Sports stars)
    ISBN 0-516-04388-9
        1. Ewing, Patrick Aloysius, 1962- –Juvenile literature.
    2. Basketball players–United States–Biography–Juvenile literature.
    3. New York Knickerbockers (Basketball team)–Juvenile literature.
    I. Title. II. Series.
    GV884.E9R366   1994
    796.323'092–dc20
    [B]   94-14399
                                                                CIP
                                                                AC

PATRICK EWING
CENTER OF ATTENTION

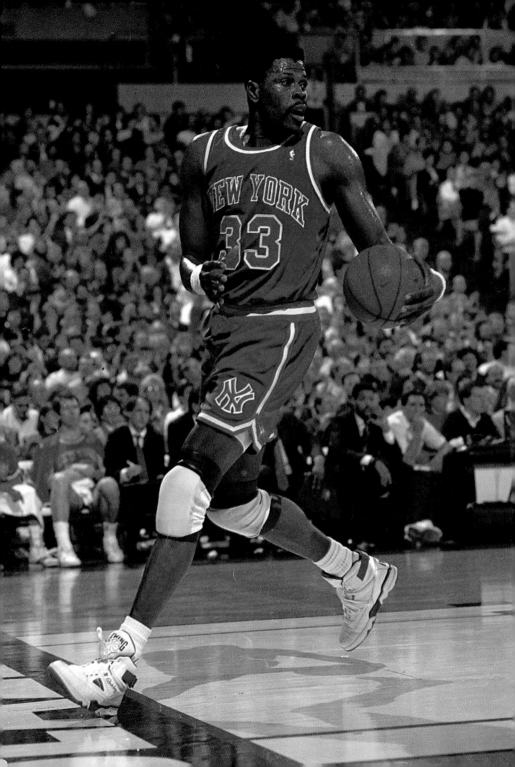

He scored a 12-foot jump shot with 1:20 left in the game. He then blocked a shot, got a rebound, and made two foul shots with 4.4 seconds remaining.

The New York Knicks had beaten the Boston Celtics by just three points, and Patrick Ewing was again a hero. As the elated crowd at Madison Square Garden cheered the Knicks off the floor, they knew that Patrick was the key to the victory. Just like in so many other victories, Patrick made the big shots.

"Patrick is the key to the offense," says Knicks' scout and former coach Fuzzy Levane. "He is the best offensive big man I have ever seen. No big man has ever been able to shoot like Patrick."

Lou Carnesecca, the retired St. John's University basketball coach, offers equally warm words of praise for the 7-foot, 245-pound center.

"I never thought I would be cheering for this guy," laughs Carnesecca, who coached four years against Patrick when the player starred at Georgetown University. "Patrick works very hard, and is a team player. Besides, he is a great shooter . . . a superstar."

Adds Houston Rockets superstar Hakeem Olajuwon: "Patrick is very physical and has tremendous talent. I admire him very much."

Patrick has certainly become one of the National Basketball Association's most admired players. But for all his success, Patrick feels his career is still not complete. He has not won an NBA championship, and no one wants to win a championship more than Patrick.

"I've won championships in high school and college, but I haven't yet won as a professional," Patrick said sadly. "I will not be satisfied until I do."

Born on August 5, 1962, in Kingston, Jamaica, Patrick was the fifth of seven children born to Carl and Dorothy Ewing. Dorothy felt there was little opportunity for success in Jamaica, and her family would be better off in America. So in 1971, she left Jamaica by herself for the United States. Patrick was only nine years old at the time.

Dorothy Ewing settled in Cambridge, Massachusetts. She got a job at Massachusetts General Hospital. As she could afford it, she sent for more of her children to join her in Cambridge. Patrick arrived on January 11, 1975. He was only 12 years old. But at 6 feet tall, he was already taller than most full-grown men.

In Jamaica, Patrick had played soccer. "I wanted to be the next Pelé," he now laughs, referring to the world-famous soccer legend.

Upon arriving in Cambridge, Patrick had never even seen a basketball. But it was not long before he started playing in the playgrounds.

Patrick learned basketball quickly as a teenager.

Georgetown University coach John Thompson scouted Patrick
when he was in high school.

Although he was tall, Patrick found that scoring baskets was a challenge. "It was tougher than I thought," he recalled.

But his skills grew quickly, like his height. He had begun to slam-dunk. By the eighth grade, he was 6 feet, 6 inches. And by his second year at Rindge and Latin High School, he was one of the best high-school players in America.

"You must see him play," Celtics president Red Auerbach told Georgetown University basketball coach John Thompson.

Thompson watched Patrick play. He quickly agreed that Patrick was a special player, one who might bring Georgetown to the top of college basketball. But Thompson would have to wait. Patrick was only a sophomore in high school.

In 1981, Patrick moved to Washington, D.C., to attend Georgetown University.

$\star\ \star\ \star$

Patrick went on to a fabulous high-school basketball career. He led his team to three state championships. He was also the only high-school player invited to try out for the United States' 1980 Olympic basketball team.

When Patrick began considering colleges to attend, his coach wrote letters to 150 colleges and universities. In February 1981, Georgetown's John Thompson visited the Ewing family. Thompson impressed the Ewings with his honesty. Before the meeting had ended, it was agreed that Patrick would attend Georgetown. Thompson would be his basketball coach. It was a decision Patrick has never regretted.

Says Patrick, "Through his leadership and guidance, Coach Thompson helped me grow as a person."

Patrick was an All-American at Georgetown for three years. He was the Big East Conference "Player of the Year" in all four of his college seasons, and he was voted best college player in 1985 by the nation's coaches.

"He's a warrior," marveled Coach Thompson, and Patrick lived up to the praise. Every year's NCAA tournament is like a brutal war, and Patrick led Georgetown to the NCAA championship game three times. Ewing's crowning achievement was 1984, when the Hoyas won the national championship and Patrick was Most Valuable Player of the tournament.

But Patrick's mother could not share in his joy. She had passed away before the start of Patrick's junior year.

Patrick celebrates with his Hoya teammates in the closing
seconds of the 1984 NCAA championship game.

After Georgetown won the championship, Patrick played for the United States men's basketball team in the 1984 Summer Olympics in Los Angeles, California. Patrick dunked the ball, blocked shots, and yanked down dramatic rebounds as the U.S. team won a gold medal.

After the Olympics, Patrick could have made a lot of money by leaving college early and playing in the NBA. But he was not interested. Patrick was determined to keep a promise he had made to his mother. He vowed that he would graduate from college.

"It's also important that we win a second straight national championship," Patrick added.

Georgetown did not win a second straight title. The Hoyas were a great team, but in the final game they were upset by Villanova, 66-64.

When the game ended, Patrick and his teammates were devastated, but they were also respectful competitors. As Villanova celebrated on the court, the Hoyas stood by and applauded the team that had defeated them.

Patrick's last college game was the 1985 NCAA championship game against Villanova.

Knick's general manager Dave DeBusschere made Patrick the
top pick in the 1985 draft.

Despite Georgetown's loss, John Thompson was proud of his team. He said, "I don't want my team to make excuses. We know how to win. We must also know how to lose."

The NBA's New York Knicks, meanwhile, knew a lot about losing. In the 1984-85 season, New York had posted a pathetic 24-58 record. The Knicks knew they had to improve their team. So they chose Patrick with the top pick in the college draft. Patrick signed a $30 million, 10-year contract, making him one of the highest paid athletes in history.

"I don't want to get used to losing," said Patrick as he prepared for his rookie year. He went on to average 20 points a game that year, and he made the All-Star team. But after suffering a string of injuries, knee surgery ended his season early. Even though Patrick had played only half a season, he was voted Rookie of the Year.

Patrick averaged 21.5 points with 147 blocked shots in his second season. But aside from Patrick's performance, these were still dismal times for the New York Knicks. They finished 24-58 in each of Patrick's first two seasons. Injuries continued to limit his playing time.

Patrick had good reason to look ahead to his third NBA campaign. After months of intense training, his knee was finally feeling better. And the Knicks had a new coach, Rick Pitino. There was a new spirit in New York. Coach Pitino introduced a new, faster-paced style of play. Patrick's knee withstood the beating of a full season — he played every game. And best of all, the Knicks made the playoffs for the first time in four years.

The thrill of the playoffs was soon dimmed, however, as the Boston Celtics eliminated New York in the opening playoff round. The Knicks still felt proud of their achievements. They knew they were a young team on the rise.

1988-89 was a breakthrough season for the Knicks. New York finished in first place in the NBA's Atlantic Division. They hadn't finished first since the championship year of 1973.

In his fourth season, Patrick set new career highs with 22.7 points a game and 281 blocked shots. He was voted to the All-NBA and All-Defensive teams, but his personal honors were overshadowed by a disappointing post-season. In the second round of the playoffs, the Knicks faced the Chicago Bulls, who were led by Michael Jordan. New York tried to out-muscle Chicago, but they could not stop Jordan. The Bulls won a thrilling series, and eliminated Patrick and the Knicks.

Michael Jordan steals the ball from Patrick; Jordan's Bulls stole a playoff series from the Knicks in 1989.

After four intense NBA seasons, Patrick's
ailing right knee could no longer stand the
punishment. In the summer of 1989, he had
knee surgery. Pro athletes are often afraid of
major surgery because the operation sometimes
takes a lot out of them. Many major stars have
failed to come back after knee or elbow surgery.

Patrick did come back in 1989-90, and he
was better than ever. New head coach Stu
Jackson brought a new twist to the Knicks
offense: pass the ball to Patrick. The results
were astounding. Patrick had a monster season.
He averaged 28.6 points and set career highs
in total points, blocked shots, and rebounds.
He firmly established himself as the best
center in basketball.

Patrick is the center of attention – even off the court.

But once again, the team could not match the accomplishments of its leader. The Knicks slid back to third place in the standings. In the playoffs, they were eliminated in the second round by the Detroit Pistons.

While the Pistons went on to win their second straight championship that summer, Patrick won his own big prize. He married Georgetown University law student Rita Williams.

The Knicks' failure to become a dominant team had begun to make Patrick unhappy. In 1990-91, yet another new coach took over the team, John McLeod. It was another outstanding season for Patrick, but another disappointing year for the Knicks. In the off-season, Patrick and the Knicks management argued over his contract. Patrick nearly left the Knicks to play for another team. The dispute went to court, and a judge ruled in the Knicks favor, blocking Patrick from becoming a free agent.

The 1991-92 season began on a fresh and optimistic note. The Knicks' new coach was Pat Riley, who had led the Los Angeles Lakers to several championships as head coach. Patrick and star teammates Charles Oakley, Gerald Wilkins, and Xavier McDaniel were all playing in the primes of their careers. Both fans and players truly believed this would be the Knicks' year.

It turned out to be a glorious regular season as the Knicks posted 51 wins. They knocked off the Pistons in the playoffs, but in the Eastern Conference Finals, they could not get past the Chicago Bulls. The Bulls were on their way to their second straight championship. Although the Knicks extended the series to a full seven games, Chicago prevailed.

Patrick and new coach Pat Riley proved to be a winning combination.

Patrick (far right) poses with fellow Dream Teamers Scottie Pippen, Charles Barkley, coach Chuck Daley, and Chris Mullin (left to right).

Patrick went to the Olympics for a second time in the summer of 1992. He was the starting center for the "Dream Team," and he was thrilled to play alongside superstars Michael Jordan, Charles Barkley, and Scottie Pippen. The U.S. team won the gold medal easily.

In the 1992-93 regular season, Patrick and the Knicks continued to establish themselves as one of the premier NBA teams, winning 60 games. Patrick averaged 24.2 points and 12.1 rebounds, and the New York fans were convinced he should be named the league's Most Valuable Player. As the last game of the season wound down, the Madison Square Garden crowd chanted, "M.V.P. . . . M.V.P." After the game, Patrick said, "It's nice the fans think I am the M.V.P."

Said Coach Riley, "Patrick is a warrior. He should be the Most Valuable Player."

But the award eluded Patrick once again. He finished fourth in the voting behind winner Charles Barkley. Knicks' forward Anthony Mason said, "I couldn't believe Patrick finished fourth. Patrick deserved to win."

Patrick was not angry. But he was upset that the Knicks once again lost to the Bulls in the Eastern Conference Finals. Everything had been going the Knicks' way early in the series. This year, New York had the home-court advantage, and they even won the first two games of the series at the Garden. But the Bulls staged a shocking comeback to win four straight games from the Knicks. Chicago then proceeded to grab its third straight NBA title.

Patrick Ewing later said, "We should have beaten them." He was tired of watching his friends on other teams battle in the NBA

In 1993, the Bulls again blocked Patrick and the Knicks from advancing in the playoffs.

Finals, while he again did not get a shot at a championship ring. The bitter taste of losing remained with Patrick for many months.

The next season began with Patrick Ewing rising to the top of the heap: on December 16, 1993, Patrick scored his 14,618th career point, becoming the Knicks' all-time leading scorer. He broke the record that had been held by Hall-of-Famer Walt Frazier.

He achieved this feat on his home floor, Madison Square Garden. Later he said, "This means a lot to me. . . . As a kid you dream of something like this, but most of my dreams are team-oriented. I'm glad it's over, but I'm very honored."

Walt Frazier understood Patrick's sense of pride in becoming the Knicks' scoring champion. But Frazier added, "What does it mean if you don't win a championship?"

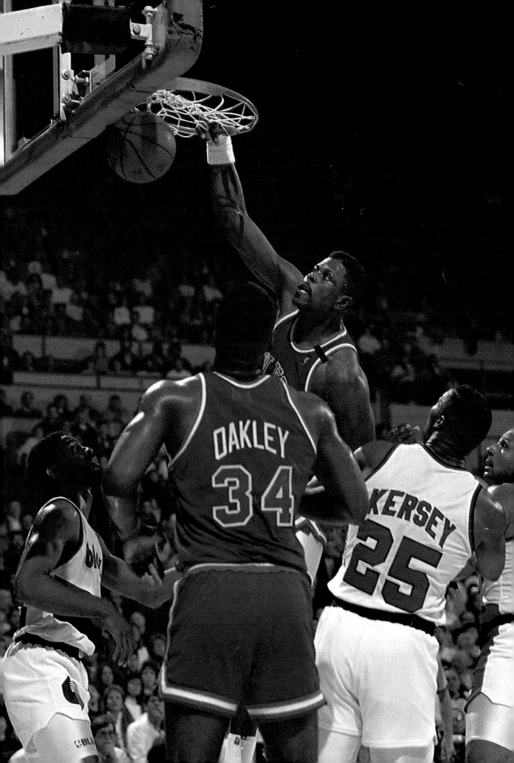

That same season, Patrick and the Knicks
moved one giant step closer to a championship.
Michael Jordan had retired from basketball
before the 1993-94 season, so the Knicks were
finally able to defeat the Bulls in the playoffs.
In the Eastern Conference Finals, they survived
a seven-game battle with the Indiana Pacers.
And for the first time in his career, Patrick had
reached the NBA Finals.

Facing the Knicks in the Finals were the
Houston Rockets, led by '93-'94 MVP Hakeem
Olajuwon. The series turned out to be a war-like
seven games, with each contest decided in the
final minutes. The Knicks won Game Five at
Madison Square Garden for a 3-2 advantage.
They could have clinched the championship
with one more victory. But the series went back
to Houston, where the Rockets won the last
two games. A heartbroken Patrick said, "I'm
extremely disappointed in the fact that we didn't
win a championship. But I still feel pride in my
teammates."

In 1994, Hakeem Olajuwon stopped Patrick from achieving his highest goal: an NBA championship.

Ewing dunks over Philadelphia's Shawn Bradley . . . who is six inches taller than Patrick!

Patrick lives in Potomac, Maryland, during the off-season. He says his parents had the biggest influence upon his life, and he wishes his mother were still alive to watch him excel in the NBA.

During games, Patrick wears a mean-looking scowl upon his face. But off the court, he smiles easily, has a sense of humor, and enjoys music. The most important thing in his life is spending time with his wife and family (son Patrick, Jr., and daughter, Randi).

Patrick is also deeply concerned with the civil rights movement in America. He says if he could have dinner with anyone in history, it would be Rev. Martin Luther King, Jr., and Malcolm X. And if he were not a basketball player, Patrick says he would have likely become an artist.

Some superstars who reach Patrick's status begin thinking so highly of themselves that they have no time to spend with their teammates. But Patrick is an outstanding team player. He always encourages his teammates — even those who rarely play.

"He is a great person," said David Cain, who played for the Knicks during the 1993 pre-season. "He took me under his wing. He helped me a lot."

Red Holtzman adds, "Patrick is a superstar who works hard and sets a wonderful example. He is a role model."

Patrick appreciates the praise. He also appreciates the importance of the two world championship rings worn by Holtzman. As Patrick always says, he won't be satisfied until he owns at least one of his own championship rings.

Chronology

1962 – Patrick Aloysius Ewing is born in Kingston, Jamaica, on August 5, 1962, the son of Carl and Dorothy Ewing.

1975 – Patrick leaves Jamaica and joins his mother in Cambridge, Massachusetts. He soon begins playing basketball for the first time.

1981 – The 7-foot Patrick leads Rindge and Latin High School to its third straight state championship.

1981-82 – Patrick wins his first of four Big East "Player of the Year" awards, and leads Georgetown University to the final game of the NCAA tournament.

1982-83 – Patrick wins his first of three All-American honors.

1984 – Patrick leads Georgetown to the NCAA championship and is voted Most Valuable Player in the NCAA tournament.
– Patrick helps America's basketball team win a gold medal in the Summer Olympics in Los Angeles, California.

1985 – Patrick is the first pick in the NBA college draft. He signs a contract with the New York Knicks that makes him one of the highest paid athletes of all time.

1985-86 – Patrick averages 20 points a game for the Knicks, makes the All-Star team, and is voted Rookie of the Year.

1987-88 – Patrick averages 20.2 points a game, leading New York to its first playoff berth in four years.

1988-89 – Patrick is voted to the All-NBA and All-Defensive teams, as the Knicks finish first in their division. Patrick averages 22.7 points a game.

1991-92 – Averaging 24 points and 11.3 rebounds a game, Patrick helps lead the Knicks to 51 regular season victories, and a first-round playoff victory over the Detroit Pistons.

1992 – Patrick helps the United States basketball Dream Team to a gold medal at the Summer Olympics in Barcelona, Spain.

1992-93 – Patrick averages 24.2 points a game, leading the Knicks to a first-place finish in the Eastern Conference. The Knicks also win 60 regular season games, tying their best season high. But they lose to the Chicago Bulls in the playoffs.

1993 – December 16: In a game against the Los Angeles Lakers, Patrick becomes the Knicks' all-time leading scorer, surpassing the record of 14,617 held by Walt Frazier.

1994 – Patrick and the Knicks finally make the NBA Finals, but are defeated by the Houston Rockets, 4-games-to-3. In the Finals, Patrick averages 18.9 points and 12.4 rebounds a game.

About the Author

Howard Reiser has been a well-known New York City newspaper reporter, columnist, and bureau chief. He has also worked as a labor news writer and editor. Today a political speechwriter, Mr. Reiser covered the major news stories in New York City for more than twenty-five years.

Mr. Reiser has written several other books in the Sports Stars series. He and his wife, Adrienne, live in New York. They have four children: Philip, Helene, Steven, and Stuart.